Genre Folktale

Essential Question
What is a folktale?

Rabbit Tricks Crocodile

A Retelling of a Japanese Folktale

retold by Pamela Walker • illustrated by Gustavo Mazali

Chapter 1
Rabbit's Wish..........................2

Chapter 2
Rabbit and Crocodile Play..............5

Chapter 3
The Trick.............................9

Respond to Reading..................12

PAIRED READ Poetry/Song: Fish School 13

Chapter 1
Rabbit's Wish

Once upon a time, Rabbit lived on a small island. Each day she stood at the edge of the shore and looked across the water.

Rabbit wished she could visit the mainland. But she could not swim.

One day, a crocodile swam by. Rabbit waved at him. "Hello, Crocodile!" she cried.

Crocodile saw Rabbit. He walked across the sand to greet her.

"I like your home," said Crocodile.

"You have a wide, sandy shore and so many bright flowers!"

"It's a nice island," Rabbit said.
"But one day I hope to live on the mainland."

"I have been there," said Crocodile.

"It's so busy, and no one wants to play. This place is much nicer."

Chapter 2
Rabbit and Crocodile Play

Crocodile spotted a round stone and pushed it with his snout. The stone rolled across the soft sand.

"This is a fun game!" cried Crocodile. "Let's roll the stone!"

Rabbit and Crocodile had lots of fun. They rolled the stone and chased it.

"Do you know any more games?" asked Crocodile.

Rabbit thought about this. "I like to hop across the sand! I hop as fast as I can!"

Crocodile frowned. "I cannot hop," he said. "You hop, and I will run!"

Rabbit and Crocodile had lots of fun. They hopped and ran across the sand.

At last, Rabbit and Crocodile stopped. They sat under a tree.

"Rabbit, I am happy we are friends," said Crocodile.

Rabbit agreed. Then she asked, "Crocodile, do you think it is good to help friends?"

"Yes, I do," said Crocodile.

"Then will you carry me on your back to the mainland?" asked Rabbit.

"No!" said Crocodile. "If you leave this island we cannot play together. You must stay here."

Chapter 3
The Trick

After a while, Rabbit asked another question. "Crocodile, are there more rabbits or crocodiles in the world?"

"There are many more crocodiles than rabbits!" replied Crocodile.

"Do you think there are enough crocodiles to stretch from here to the mainland?" Rabbit asked.

"Of course!" shouted Crocodile. He told Rabbit that he would call his friends together and prove it.

Crocodile slipped into the water. In minutes, hundreds of crocodiles joined him.

They lined up tail to snout. They soon formed a bridge that stretched from the island to the mainland.

"I must count the crocodiles to be sure," said Rabbit.

"One, two, three!" she counted. Rabbit hopped and counted across all the crocodiles.

Soon she hopped over the last one. Then Rabbit took one final, giant hop.

At last, Rabbit reached the mainland! She waved goodbye to Crocodile as she got ready to explore!

Retell

Use your own words to retell *Rabbit Tricks Crocodile*.

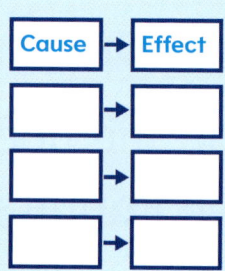

Text Evidence

1. Look at pages 2 and 3. Why can't Rabbit go to the mainland? **Cause and Effect**

2. Look at page 8. Why won't Crocodile take Rabbit to the mainland? **Cause and Effect**

3. How do the animals in this folktale act like humans? **Genre**

Genre Poetry/Song

Compare Texts
Read a poem about a fish with a wish.

Fish School

by Pamela Walker
illustrated by Ilias Arahovitz

A blue and gold fish
jumped out of his pool.
He had just one wish,
to go to school.

Out on dry land,
Fish looked left and right.
He saw not one school,
not one school was in sight!

Back in the water
Fish swam through the blue,
wishing for a school,
crying, Boo Hoo Hoo!

And that's when he saw it,
a school just for fish!
He joined all the others
who had the same wish!

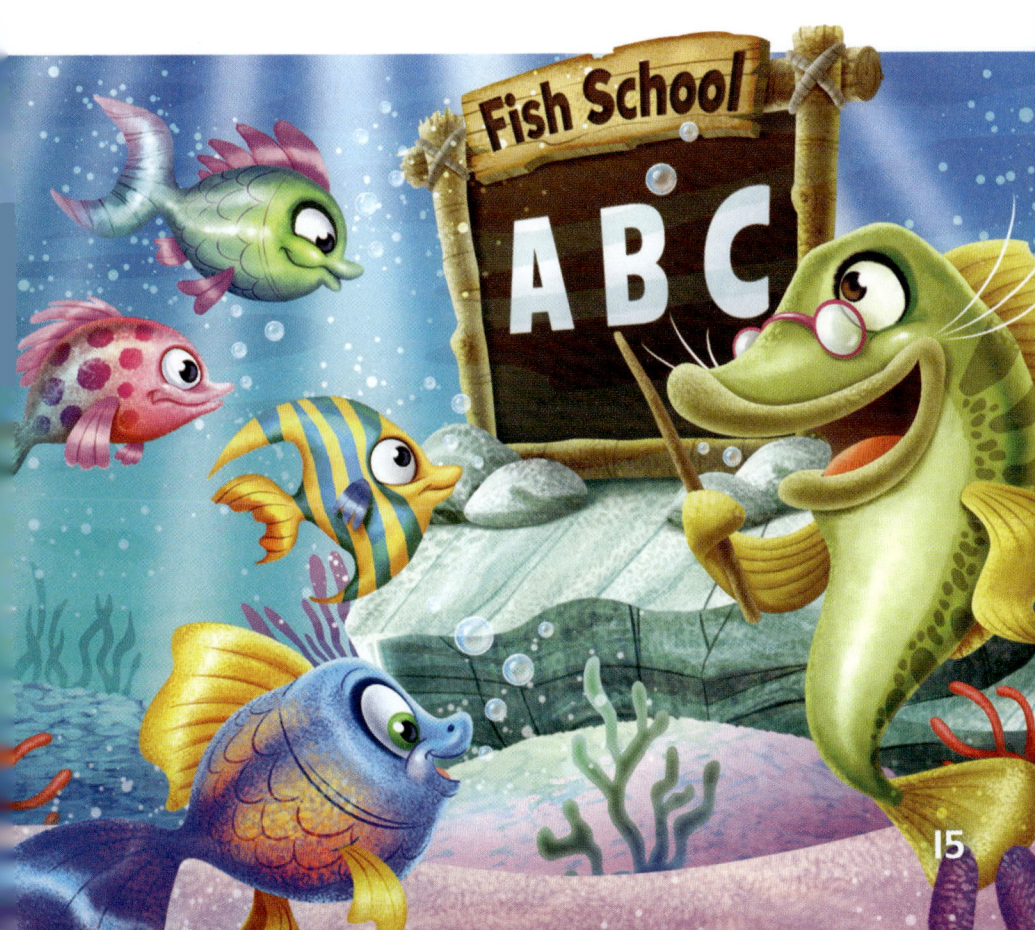

Focus on

Folktale A folktale is a story based on traditions and customs. Folktales have been passed along through the years by telling them aloud. Folktales often have characters that speak and act like humans.

What to Look for In *Rabbit Tricks Crocodile,* Rabbit and Crocodile talk and act like people. Rabbit tricks Crocodile to help her get to the mainland. In real life, animals don't do these things.

Your Turn

Write a folktale about an animal character that tricks another animal. Draw a picture to go with your story. Share your folktale and drawing with the class.